intoxicated heart

ben esqueda

dear world,

this is me. this book holds my happiest memories and it also holds my raw 3am thoughts that made me feel like the darkest soul. this is the first time i didn't ignore how my heart felt. i was scared to love at first, as anyone would be. healing a broken heart can be one of the challenging chapters in your life, as it was for me. there is something so poisonous yet so beautiful about not being able to control your love for another human. to say i fell in love with you would be an understatement. you were the fuel to my heart, our 3am conversations made sleep feel pointless, and i swear i could have spent a lifetime getting lost in your eyes. we were young and somehow our love turned into lust. we both made decisions without realizing the consequences, and here we are now just as we started, as strangers. the bad outweighed the good in you, and i still couldn't stop myself from your touch. i was blinded by your love and hoped your promising lies would somehow turn into truth. i ignored reality and ran with our tainted dreams, and eventually i started to feel my foundation burn down. you left without a reason, and it made me believe i wasn't good enough. so this is where my heart started writing about our memories, my heartache, and how i recovered from you. it took months to feel the sun again, but i am back and stronger than i've ever been. it all begins with yourself, everything and anything. self-care is so vital—watch a sunset, nourish your soul with your own water. i wrote down every single thought that snuck into my nightmares at night. and after all the chaos, you are just a black hole covered by a heart. to all of you reading this, i hope one poem can change your life in some form whether it be to give goosebumps because it brought back a beautiful memory or because it reminded you of a dark time and it made you realize that you got through it. i want you to understand that you can find your way out of the darkness, that it's okay to feel, and most of all to know you have a purpose on this earth.

first sip of you

this world has been alive for 4.51 billion years
and we happened to be born during the same time
but we still have an entire world around us
yet we somehow met, connected
and showed each other a new light

i opened my eyes
and rolled over to find you
intertwined in my sheets
not only in my dreams
but now on earth
i was living about half right
until you walked in my heart
with your light
clear skies and no more thunder
you turned my insomnia into slumber

dance floor love

kissing under the disco
never held onto a body so tight
nothing has ever felt more right
song ended and we drifted outside
just me and you with a night sky view
i can't keep my hands off you
when our lips touch
it's like you knew the rhythm of my soul

a new heart
a chance to love again, a new start
a new pair of eyes
they scream so bright and wise
and a new set of hands
a new grip, a new fit

the perfect date

the simplicity of doing absolutely nothing yet were talking up a storm. the world feels like it's at a pause but our hearts are racing faster than ever. your energy with mine is the perfect blend of nostalgia and ease.

i've always wanted to travel the world
i met you
and saw the world in your eyes
then suddenly i became a body of butterflies
you put out the fires in my forest

i'm in love with the way you look at life
the way you look at the clouds
the way your eyes light up for coffee
the way your heart hurts for others
you've taught me
how to find the colors in every moment
when all i see used to see
was black and white
you've taught me
how to light a fire in my heart
and let it burn at its full capacity
thanks to you,
i live in a new galaxy

it's as if
your fingertips struck me with lightning
every time they touched my body
it's as if
your kisses were the wind
that blew away my storms
it's as if
your eyes were the sun
that scared away my shadows

it was a new kind of love
you chose to give me a new heart
instead of repairing the damage
you chose to create new memories
instead of repeating the old

it was you
the way your fingers locked into mine
felt like a new galaxy was born and exploding
all at the same time
the moment our eyes connected
i felt the rush of warmth in my body
the way our lips touched
the way the world stopped
it felt like the only thing that existed was you and i
it's 3am now and my lips are still locked on yours
i feel electricity striking through in and out of our bodies
it was you
it was love

you and i
something i have never felt
it was better than any dream i could imagine
it was a dream on earth
our talks about life
our laughs and fights
everyone enjoys stargazing
but the second i looked into your eyes
i knew you were my favorite star
something you've never felt
you and i

i remember that night under the sky
us just laying there
staring into the silence of the stars
feeling like i heard a symphony
coming from mars
this was the night
where all the walls
came crashing down
the ocean
and the stars
they played us a magic show

i traveled to the messiest
and darkest
parts of your mind
and found light
in the cracks and crevices
of your heart

my mother always told me
to stay where the sun shines
i met you
& you were the warmth of the sun
i never experienced

i always replay our memories in my head
the memories that cleared my mind
and made me feel as if
everything before us
didn't matter
our hearts are intertwined
hands locked like a special design

it's all because you remind me
of my hometown
the warmth you gave
the comfort of your touch
the joy i saw inside your eyes
it's not about what you did
but how you made me feel
you made my soul feel like
a starlit sea of life
when it used to feel like
an undiscovered dark sea

intoxicated heart

it was our first kiss
the night sky never looked brighter
it was so cold
but,
i was next to you warmer than i've ever been
i gently ran my fingers
through your hair
i grabbed your face
and i couldn't help myself

stay with me
keep your clothes on
undress your heart
take a deep breath
and show me your secret art

your blood was so warm
like heated silver and salt
melt in my arms
your lips
my lips
let's unfold
and create gold

a night sky view and a bottle of wine
if i said this wasn't a perfect date
i would be lying
laughs that turned into crying
we paused for a moment
just to admire each other's eyes
they were glowing
and the momentum was flowing

your voice was harmony to my ears
our memories felt like a movie
i keep replaying them in my head
the sweet things
that come out of your mouth
stuck on the alluring words
you once said
that felt like poetry

it's 4:17 am
it's more windier than usual
and rain magically appeared
just like how you appeared in my life
my goosebumps vanished
when you wrapped your arms around me
like a bandage
your hair in my face
feels so annoyingly perfect

intertwining souls
we can't stop this feeling
we're looking like fools
when i'm with you
it feels like a dream on repeat
i can smell, hear, and taste
our memories
they are so clear

when i try to list
the reasons why i fell for you
there are no words
that could explain the emotions
that were being stirred
while my heart was wrapped around yours
it was just a feeling
that made my fireworks go off

the morning came too soon
last night was my favorite full moon
we woke up to the sound of city streets
and the sun that reflected off the sheets
i leaned into whisper those three words
just a short moment of love within

you stole my heart
through your fingertips
that gently played that song
on the piano
your cherry red lips
in the most romantic dim light
i couldn't help myself but take a bite

this dark loving at night
all these crazy bars
and we somehow always
ended up at the beach
staring at the stars

that malibu night
started with trying your ice cream
i would look at you
and internally scream
then dived right into your angelic face
the ice cream tasted better on your lips
never ending kisses and grips
this is the best type of apocalypse

i thought i wasn't capable of loving someone
the minute i walked in the door i felt it
it's like my heart instantly exploded
like it hasn't been alive in years
you made me feel my changed heart

racing through the city
your touch lit me up
like a never-ending fire
we talked about the first day we met
and eventually caught the sunset
we took a taxi to the tallest view
in the backseat now
hands on your thigh
if i were to tell you i didn't fall for you
it would be a lie

if the lights turned on
and the door opened
then the world saw
we would convince them that we belong

lost in lust
past midnight

your heartbeat
your touch
your lips
your eyes
it's like i saw the whole universe
in your eyes
and i'm lost in it

chests pressed against one another
hearts beating against each other
so offbeat yet so on tune
you've become my favorite muse

you know you have fallen for someone when
every piece of light
and every piece of darkness
in them
is all a masterpiece to you

when you rather talk to someone
instead of sleep
you know you have fallen
fallen so hard
be careful though
because when you choose a human
over sleep
you might end up choosing
lust over
love

i hate the way you grab my face
and make it all feel like
your heart is my home
your touch is my comfort
your smile is my sun
and your freckles are
my night sky of stars

it all sounds so stupid
4am
doors locked and lights off
two bodies in one bed
your fingertips gently brushing across my chest
this was the night feelings were confessed
you whispered in my ear
something you love most about me
was the freckles on my shoulders
it sounds so stupid but i thought to myself
how can my biggest insecurity
be your favorite thing

you looked at me like i was meant for you
i looked at you and didn't know what to do
i was afraid of giving me to you
story of my life

as soon as i parked my car
my favorite view wasn't far
we jumped straight to the back seat
lip biting and tight grips
suddenly my teeth in your neck
still wasn't close enough to you
it was a dangerous time
and we both knew

i guess the part that hurts me the most is
you will never see me the way i see you
the second we exchanged love i knew,
i knew my life was going to turn upside down
and i was somehow okay with it

meeting you was like
running into the most alluring room
my eyes have ever seen
then you turned the lights off
and locked me in

months later my heart still raced
as i was about to see your face
it's almost as if you walked in slow motion
a perfect image
that i can't help but chase
grab my hand
and let's dance at your pace

and i hate you

but i only hate you because

i love you

the way you would throw your head back when you laughed

the way you looked into me

the way i fell for you

the way i can't stop falling

from this never-ending ledge

i hate you

our love story
was like a car ride at 100 miles per hour
we weren't wearing seat belts
we knew the consequences
we knew it was a dead end

the issue with me is
i search for peace
in a place full of hate
and constantly looking at a place
that looks like heaven
but inside of it is hell

i saw your eyes
and saw endless love
in a place
that never had a starting line

we have our favorite love songs on
with no idea on how to love each other

i can see your soul
ignite with light
in pitch black
your mind is so cloudy
you can't see the sun
but i'm finding you
i'm for you
i'll make that heart flutter
once more

i tasted love on your lips
and felt lust in your hips
i'm confused
i want you in ways
i never wanted anyone

i'm holding onto a memory
a memory that made me forget
about the past extravagant
moments in life
listen,
you weren't extravagant
you didn't even need to speak.
the sparks in your eyes
and the stars that arise
finding the missing puzzle pieces
to your heart
that's what i'm holding onto

perhaps when we met we were broken
but we didn't know it
but what we thought we knew
was that we were in love
we couldn't resist each other's energy
to the point where it was toxic

my mom warned me about your type of drug
i promised her i would never try it
you see,
i wasn't aware that you were that drug
what i thought was
the happy ending to my book
the missing piece to my heart
the island i never knew existed
but hold up
wait a minute
i got it all twisted
you slipped the drug on your lips
the moment they touched
i was in some other world
i'm craving your lips on mine
you are my drug addiction

back and forth
with the constant games
starting to make me feel a little insane
it's almost as if
i have to act like i hate you
in order for you to like me

it's not intentional
i don't mean to play your game
i know i deserve better
i know i shouldn't be texting you
but sometimes at night
i want to know
if you're alright

time is ticking
and my feelings are sinking
beneath the sea
endless nights of games
and deep conversations
that lead to nothing
when i wake up in the morning

sucker for your touch
all it took was one night
and now i'm left with this
unexplainable feeling
i had no idea
that you would be
the ocean to my ears
when i fall asleep
and now i'm feeling fear
because how can something be
so poisonous be yet so beautiful

little did you know
i was tongue tied in my words
scared to look in your eyes
nervous to lock hands
and feared i would fall for you
little did you know

you have that mysterious touch to your eyes
i'm falling in love with your lies
late night car rides
you and i
playing our late night tunes
making me feel like i'm forever on a honeymoon
running my fingers through your hair
ah, my favorite nightmare

when you hold onto someone
who doesn't know how to hold onto you
it will slowly but surely
cause you to lose yourself

wrapped up in between
fighting for a love
that might cause me
to lose myself
or
lose you
and fight for me

in search for a sober mind again
you were never prescribed to me
i told myself it was just one night
and here i am
overdosing on your touch

you felt yourself

going under the covers

you felt a feeling

that you never knew existed

you allowed yourself to feel for someone

who doesn't feel for you

turn off the light
crawl into my bed
and get inside my head
1 2 3
kiss
1 2 3
tongue tied
1 2 3
this is what it feels like to collide

it seems as if
you only miss me
when the sun goes down
when i'm with you
everything around us
is a ghost town
while kissing you
feels like i'm in my hometown

maybe i've done the crime
maybe i caught you in your lies
maybe your lies have me crazy
i haven't been myself lately

let's tear apart the surface
and seduce me
with your mind and soul
tell me everything you want to be
and why you hate rock and roll
show me your concept of love
and what makes your heart whole

broken bottles and insomnia

i know i came off cold
but darling
i swear there is a raging fire
somewhere in between
the holes in my soul
heart skipping three beats at once
it's been months

when you hold me, my mind sets free
in a blink of an eye
our entire story was a lie
i play piano to clear my head
it feels like the love you once had for me
is dead

as i sit
it all hit
was your love real?
please tell me the truth
it's the only way i'll heal

you introduced yourself to me
in black and white
and i still saw all the colors you carried
do me a favor,
stop living your life half awake
and let's nourish your heart ache
my heart is at war for you

ah love,
the warmth that can make you feel out of this world
an explosion of unexplainable emotion
a sudden touch from them is like
lightning striking and running through your body
but,
it's also the passion that can make you feel
under and alone in this world
an explosion of unexplainable emotion
a sudden touch that once made you feel electric
is now kicking you to the ground
and making you feel sick

you came into my life unexpectedly
and you left just the same
i should've known all it was
was a game

i listened to your lies
knowing you were lying
i absorbed your lies
and hoped they would turn into truth

yesterday you were inside my bed
today you're across the world from me
and now just memories in my head
i would do anything
to kiss your forehead
and whisper nonsense in your ears again

the clock hit midnight
i'm starting to feel my bruised mind
caving emotions into paper
because our hearts are no longer aligned

does he wipe your tears away the way i do?
or does he let them dry?
does he tell you the truth the way i do?
or does he lie like you too?

it's 365/365
my mind is done
but my heart puts you first
before anyone
my mind
and my heart
are in a warzone

"come on and let loose, it's fun"
the moment i recognized
the bottle in your hand
snatched your mask off
that's when i saw the real you
and you were no longer
a pleasant view

the way i push you away
convincing myself we grew apart
then seconds later pull you in
to cure my artificial heart
is this how i'm supposed to heal?
is this how i'm supposed to feel?

we connected
we created a galaxy together
we created an uninvented feeling
we get locked in each other's eyes
you had me
and i had you
then we disconnected
then our galaxy exploded
then that uninvented feeling we once had
was reinvented with someone else
now you are locked in their eyes
lost in trying to find yourself
in someone else

we so often
fight for a love
that's not worth fighting for
if only knowledge
was put in front of our hearts
we wouldn't battle and we would understand
that the best thing for us
is to be apart

you tell me i'm your everything
but treat me like i'm your nothing
i'm fighting for you
while you're in a different war
fighting for someone else

i struggle to forget
but for you
it's as if
we never met

your lips

feel like a lust potion

your lies

feel like they will end up being truth

loving you

feels like a crime

losing you

feels like i'm attempting to become sober

it's been some time now
how can i escape you
when the only thing i think about is you
is this how i'm supposed to heal?
forcing myself to starve my heart
when the only thing it craves is you

as i close my eyes at night
i pray once more
to let my eyes see the light
i can't see the stars
i pray once more
to take away the clouds
i'm writing about you
i pray once more
to take away the thunderstorm
you caused

i'm still driving on the road you once showed me
you promised me
you would be waiting for me
at the end of the road
i'm still driving on the road you once showed me
full of life and green surroundings
and the more i drive
the deader things are looking
i'm still driving on the road you once showed me
and i'm starting to think you aren't
waiting for me
and there is no ending to the road

on the days
where i forget to drink all of my coffee
and write a little extra about you
wondering what went wrong
and how having no closure is like
a half-written story
finished,
without and ending

writing away through the hours
staring at the walls during timeless showers
my ten fingers, two hands, and one pair
writing about a story i imagined
when all along it was
dead magic and one sided passion

praying for peace in my mind
but to say you aren't the last thing
i think about at night
i would be lying

deep breath
one month
deep breath
two months
deep breath
three months
it will get better
it will get brighter
it takes time
just know it will get easier

i want to be with you at 3am
when i know i'm not supposed to
i feel this love for you
when i know i'm not supposed to
i want to unravel your heart
when i know i'm not supposed to
so i'll just sit back and pretend
i forget to text you back

i seem to catch myself
falling for people
and caring for others
when they don't know how to
care for themselves

just because you are good for someone
doesn't mean they are good for you

we sat in your car
you played music
my unsaid feelings
somehow spilled out of your mouth
and in that very moment
my gate opened for you
but over time
as feelings flowed
they flowed in other ways
and now i'm here
waiting for you to return
it feels like
sending a balloon to you
in the sky
hoping it will get to you

belly aches and headaches
dark thoughts and twisted stomach nots
all caused by an individual
that promised to show me a life of love

i fall
and i fall again
and right when i think
it can't get darker
i find a new shade of black
my mind is in a permanent flashback
of what we could've been
and what we really were

you started this fire in me
a new color
a new flame
you are watching my heart ignite
i can feel my heartache
twice as bad at night

loving on long distance
you left
memories faded, love faded
and i can't remember the way your lips felt on mine
and i can't remember the way your details were designed
and i can't remember the motions of your heart
i know you better in my dreams

i wanna taste you again
my favorite secret and sin
without you
my head is in a constant spin
in what we were
and what we could've been

what a shame
you messed up
and you play the blame game
who's right
who's wrong
but don't worry because tomorrow morning
i'll be gone

body of a black hole

started as a romantic comedy
ended as a horror

i am trying to love you
because my heart is not okay without you
and,
also remember the reason i'm numb
is because of you.
it's all over in my head
but you have my heart
please don't leave it dead

i gave it all
when i mean all
i gave you my heart,
my mind,
and my flesh
but,
you gave me broken promises,
hopeless expectations,
and a dark mind
but the one thing you kept
was my heart
give it back.

it can take seconds
for your life to shatter
but years
to gather your life back together

i hate you
i hated the magical words that you said
i hated that you didn't love yourself
i hated that we were young
i hated that a compatible stash of addicting drugs
was more relatable to our story
but most of all
i hate that i love you

i'm caught up with love
love that i have for someone
when that someone doesn't even exist
you showed me someone
that was built on fiction
you make me feel crazy
because i'm caught up in you
but it isn't you
because you
aren't you

the night you saw me for me
was beautiful as can be
why did i open up to someone
when i knew deep down inside
you would turn and run
it was dark love
and now it's something
i'm just trying to let go of

if you stare long enough you can find the demon lying beneath the angel eyes

we were falling together
but i fell faster
and you learned how to fly
i'm on the ground now
and you're in the sky

i miss feeling butterflies
i miss seeing the sun in people's eyes
it seems like everyone i fall for
feeds me nothing but lies

you are so hurt

that you think darkness is light

you are so used to being mistreated

that you confuse it with love

you are so caught up in good memories

you have with someone you can't get rid of

when i wake up
i won't be in your arms
when i wake up
i'll be thousands of miles away
from your heart
physically
but mentally
i'm still infatuated with the possibility
but if i continue being your puppet
i will lose my dignity

temporary distractions
are your attractions
pick a book off the shelf
and learn how to love yourself
be your own light
when you are scared at night

darker skies
heavier eyes
and a more shallow mind than the night before

i painted my mind with
full imagination and expectation

threw my heart around
and acted like it didn't have value
how can i let go
if i never had you

i could create the perfect world
for you
and it still wouldn't be enough
just promise me
you will love yourself
the way you want people
to love you

we started as strangers
and we ended the same
the only difference is
i have a book full of memories
and feelings
that set my heart on fire
in the end

when i first met you
you were like a rare species
so stunning and so beautiful
but time revealed
that the rare parts of you
were lies
and you're just like the rest

you read me like a book
you had the perfect intro
enough to get me hooked
i should've known how it ended
you had a summary
that i wish i could amend
i thought i was your climax
but i'm not even in your book

and this whole time
i thought your heart
was like a cup of coffee in the morning

• a dangerous and dark time

tangled up in your sheets
as you're tangled in my heart
stubborn and selfish
broken and feeling less
a new body in my bed having slumber
when you're alone in your bed having nightmares
but the second you think you're getting closure
i'll get a little closer
a guilty heart with no self control
but i have control on your soul

i was climbing from the dark hole
then you came to grab my hand
and help me out the darkness
i thought
but you grabbed my hand
and showed me a new world
of darkness

how is it possible to love someone
who taught you how to hate yourself

silly me
for thinking i could
make you a better you
when at the end
you made me a worse me

my heart shifted
you lifted and i fell
at one point in time
i thought the floors and foundation we made together
was a stable place to walk and live in confidence
the marble floors had my name written all over it
and the only place i found your name
was in the cracks and corners
yes i am ashamed of who you became
but who am i to blame?

i started to see shadows in pitch black
and that's when i knew
lights off felt like comfort
rain on my skin brought me warmth
and lonely was my new best friend

chasing you was like
driving next to an airplane
as it was taking off
i'm speeding up in hopes
that my car will somehow fly next to you
when all along i always knew
i knew my car would never fly
i knew i could never get a hook in your heart

•   3am drunk text from you

i'm selfish

i'm selfish in the way i use your love

for attention, validation, and happiness

the way i use your body at night

until we see daylight

and the way i kiss your lips

for a quick fix

while imagining someone else

you were everything
my heart and mind imagined
so i gave it to you
my heart was everything you imagined
to break and wreck
after all you were just
a joker in the deck

you hid your true identity
to commit loveless acts
i had a huge fence up
but you slipped right into the cracks

and it's all because you reminded me
of the darkest time of my life
my guts are screaming at my heart
i can't play this game again
i'm not jumping into a tsunami
to end up on the floor
washed up on the shore
once more

i treat our memories
like old antiques my grandma has
and every bad thing you did to me
resembled the dust on the antiques
and i blew that dust off
and pretended we would be okay
when i knew over time
you wouldn't only create dust
but you would shatter the antiques

started as strangers
ended up as friends
i enjoyed your presence
then no strings attached
we made that second too long eye contact
and now i'm latched
and locked in your love
you were always a really good storyteller
and your story ended how it started
with being strangers

started with loyalty
and what we would call love
ended with insanity
and what we would call lust

- fiction love

repetitive months of writing
about endless dreams and endless love
dedicated to your decorated lies

sometimes i like to ask myself
if some things
will ever truly pass by
it feels as if i'm running in a circle
with no ending
laughter of fun
spark of love
the loss of feelings

will you ever fall out of it
almost like this alter ego
will you realize that there is more to life
you have a heart
i've felt it
time to time
let your heart win the battle

why do i blame it on me
your imperfections
your insecurities
your issues
i blame it on me
why am i hurting more than you
all i wanted to do
was help it all
and make you the person you dream of
but you messed up
why do i blame it on me

hands are shaking
my positive vision is fading
i can't control my plane anymore
i'm not the pilot i used to be
i can't control my plane anymore
i'm headed into the black sea

emptiness dancing in my soul
feeling like i got sucked
into a black hole
this undiscovered feeling of dark
trying to dance my way out
to find that spark

you were like a decaf cup of coffee
you looked so damn scrumptious
and tasted even better
but once i drank all of you
i still felt empty
no energy, no love

3am
the time where love has never felt more alive
your kisses on my neck
sleep felt pointless when i was next to you

3am
my internal butterflies
turned into the darkest heartache
because of your twisted lies
the time where love
has never felt more poisonous

we ripped each other up
and ended up
like a damaged masterpiece
it's time we let the old flow away
and let the new paint away
with new designs and new colors

life can switch in seconds
when you start depending
on another human
to feed you
attention, love, and validation
be careful please
the person that you are relying on
for attention
might have no intention
of caring for your heart

stop devouring the lies
like you're dying from starvation
deep down in the dark
where the pieces are of your broken heart
your heart will never stop bleeding
if you never let go of the knife

i wish i knew you

like your favorite song knows you

i wish i could cure your pain

the way those drugs did

i wish i could be your happy ever after

but you need to fall in love with yourself first

and when that day comes

maybe our souls will

accidentally reunite in a new way

but until then

i hope that song that makes your tears fall

eventually dries up

and teaches you how to smile again

hydrating the heart

so this is where i become stronger
i admit my unsaid heart-wrenching feelings
for you
to you
and i choose to stop myself
because
it isn't love that we have
i can feel it taking over my body
doing things out of dumb attraction
instead of true actions with passion
so this is where i become stronger

dear god,
as i sit alone at the beach
as i sit in peace
you show me love
when i look above
in my world there is darkness
but the more i look up i get scared less
i shut my eyes and listen to the ocean
i set my mind free
and let you take in motion

be light
don't let the darkness in the world
take away your stars
use those stars you have
and turn them into galaxies of light
open your imagination
and start your gravitation

i'm ready

i'm ready to believe you were a lesson

i'm ready to see sunshine

i'm ready to nourish my heart

i'm ready

and after all the mess
i finally feel less
i'm finally letting go
and i'm going with the flow
i know i'm worth more

find you
dig under the sadness
that was piled over your happiness
remember how it feels
true joy

you will never succeed in life
if people believe in you
more than you believe
in your self

i feel me

i feel happy

the sun is rising beneath my night sky

i can feel the warmth from this world

i can feel once again

there is something so amazing about reaching for a night sky of stars knowing you will never get to touch them. it's like a little reminder that this world has endless possibilities.

i woke up today
drank my coffee
& wrote this poem
i'm looking at life from a brighter perspective
i want to remind you to smile today
because if your life is raining
believe me
the sun will come out before you know it

there is nothing
like a dark chapter in your book
i'm sure it's a life changing chapter
but remember
let yourself evolve into a better you
learn from it
grow from it
and love it

i saw you the other night
i looked into your eyes from time to time
as time ticked
and actions moved forward
i suddenly realized
i know your name
i know a part of your story
but life happens
and people change
the ocean drifted us apart
but i wish you the best

time
it's precious
it's valuable
it's special
don't let people treat it as if it's not
it's what creates beautiful memories
it's what teaches you
how hard things can get in life
it's what shows you
how over time it will be okay

my hearts beating
i hear the birds chirping
i opened my eyes today
my heart is full
because of me
and also because
i let god take the lead

tears of joy

tears of sorrow

tears of pain

it's all emotions

live in it

learn from it

& accept it

past

my heart is cured somehow through you. i never knew the sun can come from a smile, passionate love can spark through another pair of eyes, and the galaxies i would always dream of touching are now the freckles on your body. you look at me like i'm some art piece and you listen to me like i'm some symphony from heaven. it's not that i was broken, it's more of that you showed me there is no limit to happiness. the feeling between us is like a chevy bel air cruising down the 101 freeway in los angeles. our phones were non existent like the 50's. the traffic didn't make me as bitter, music blasting and this feeling felt forever lasting. our conversations were never ending and sleep was unheard of.

present

my heart was never cured. your smile that once showed the sun is now just a dull night sky, the spark of passionate love through your eyes is now an explosion of chaos, and your galaxies of freckles are now just dots on skin. now you look at me like your world is ending and you listen to me like national emergency alert system. yes, the feeling between us was like a vintage chevy bel air but we broke down fast. my phone started to become more astonishing than the flesh in front of me and we were back in present day. conversations started to feel surfaced and i started to love my sleep again. you never noticed the rust on the hood of my heart.

there are days
when my stars
light up my sky

my inner cosmos
letting my mind expand in happiness
letting me write about my struggles
and turning it all into art

but there are also days
when my stars aren't visible

making me think i'm not worthy
making me feel hopeless
almost like i'm not going to feel
the warmth again

but let me tell you something
there is an infinite amount of joy
out there in the world
you will find it
it can't hide long
if you seek

it's important to heal the hole in your heart
that they left behind
we don't want them to ever come back in
you don't deserve holes
you deserve a garden of healthy flowers

sometimes you need to take the next step and stop writing about the person that shattered you in every way possible. they aren't worthy of your raw beautiful mind spilled onto paper anymore. don't waste your precious life on someone who chooses not to have time for you.

an accidental visit

it's been months since our last conversation. you walked in the room and i felt that same sparkling, fuzzy heart feeling when i first met you. but then i remembered the damage you caused, and after that the fuzzy heart feeling got sucked away into reality. after that, i looked into your eyes again and i felt nothing because i know i deserve everything.

in the aftermath of chaos
i learned how to breathe
on my own again
i found the beauty
in city views and the ocean again
i smile because it's over
our tragedy
is now transformed into fascinating art

you will be happy again
you will feel again
you will love again
sadness in our chapters
will always come and go

and this is where it starts to turn
my vision gets brighter
the cold isn't so cold anymore
i take my steps without hesitation
i'm putting my hands up
and i'm enjoying the ride

i love you
but i love me more
so this is where me comes
before you
and i let go

when you finally learn
to love yourself
is when you learn
that it's not about not being good enough
it's maybe about
how they weren't good enough for you

if your heart is broken:

you might have lost yourself in the midst of fighting for someone else but you lost the fight and now you need to find yourself again. please take the long way home.

coming to realization-

sometimes you need to realize
you can't wrap your arms around a memory
and those memories you're holding onto
might be with someone
that isn't that someone anymore
sometimes feelings fade
and hearts drift into different currents

i learn about myself more
the more i let you go
and i love myself more
the more i love you less

so here's the thing
i want to love you with all i have
but with the little i have
i need to love myself
and travel inside my own mind
but until i'm redesigned
be safe darling

part 1
love is fading faster
days are getting darker
our minds are becoming foggier
and we once wanted to fly
but got comfortable with floating
and some of us are even falling
then we hide in what we want to feel
because having feelings
doesn't feel normal anymore

part 2
do me a favor and close your eyes
take a trip to the mind of your own
listen to the crickets
and realize your mind has no limits
then instead of judging yourself
forgive yourself and let go
there is art living beneath your skin
and a unique light that touches people
that lives in your veins
and flows like waves
slow it down
listen to your heart
and stop planting your roses
in gardens that tear you apart
listen to your mind
realize all the time you're wasting
and stop chasing

i know one day
you're going to come back
looking for what you once
found in me
but by that time
i have found
what you found in me

i was drowning in your storm
when i thought you were teaching me
how to swim
i was so deep in the ocean
the lies were pulling me down
i didn't see the sun anymore
i saw your creatures in the ocean
down below
that i never knew existed in you
as time went on
i taught myself how to swim
i got washed up to the shore
i'm out of your storm
i look back now
and i can't see it
or feel it

it's okay to feel lost in a world where you feel the need to be found. during the time of feeling lost please focus and remember to breathe then live in the exact moment you are reading my words. feel every rain drop on your skin and let your heart flutter to love songs on the radio. be present and dig inside your mind, you have a world of your own.

you are worth so much more
you don't deserve a heavy heart
you don't deserve sleeping alone
in a bed designed for two
you deserve so much more

part 1
you were the first person
i opened my heart to
you planted your flowers
it took some time for them to grow
but in the meantime you nourished them
as time went on they bloomed
but little did i know
those thorns on your flowers
were the most poisonous things
i ever let grow in my garden

part 2
it's been some time
but your flowers are not only dead
but i pulled them from the soil
and planted my own
no thorns
no rain
and the best of all
no more pain

sober mind

to love isn't always two humans getting lost in each other's eyes.

maybe it's that night you chose to stare at the stars until sunrise.

or that one time you gave that homeless family $5 when you only had $6 to your name.

or maybe it's being kind to a human that was not the sweetest to your heart.

find love in the simple things like the sheet's you fall asleep with and the coffee you wake up to.

never love less
just because someone
couldn't love you at your most

breathe you are alive
thanks for giving me another day of life
the sun shines so bright
thanks for giving me inner light
at my lowest points i pray
thanks for showing me faith

after diving into a few hearts
that had nothing but broken promises
i finally found my own
i found the missing pieces
i found self-secure love
i found my own heart

and that's the thing about love
each time you fall in love
there is a new definition
that describes perfection
a whole new body of art
a new pitch of voice
and a new fairy tale
that you hope
has a happy ever after

i let you go
and i caught myself
as time went on my cloudy sky
poured rain
then came a rainbow
and ended with the warm sun

stories in motion-

go to a coffee shop. sit, reflect, and look around you. listen to the guy on your left playing his heart out on the piano with a tip jar next to him. feel the dim light that's setting the welcoming mood. look outside the window and notice the girl sitting on the curb crying in devastation and praying that it will get better. last but not least, move your motion to the right and take a glance at what it seems to be a couple living off young love as they race into the coffee shop. they look like they were living in a picture perfect romantic film and it's almost as if every action they made was in slow motion.

after all the chaos
i hope you choose to remember
the angels between us
and the countless sleepless nights
laughing at the absolute art of love

i'm in the car alone
seat belt buckled
i'm the only one on the road
going 100 miles per hour
i'm looking into the rearview mirror
i can't see you anymore
i can't feel you anymore
i can see gratitude again
i can feel again

gathered thoughts in clouds-

there is something so beautiful about being 35,000 feet above land, it's like my worries vanished and heaven got a little closer. there are parts of me that i didn't know exist. there are bruises in my heart that never healed properly. there are memories that have made me feel like a shooting streak of light, that are now blurry and fragmented because our world glorifies violence rather than peace. i'm learning that finding peace in a dark night of stars and diving into an ocean of crystal blue persuasion is a simplistic gift that we should all try some time.

7 years old

you kept my perception of life sweet
in a world of bitter
just a boy with
a playful heart and scabs on my knees
seven years old in the back seat
an imagination of dreams and happiness

you looked back and rolled down my window then told me to
close my eyes, open my hand, and stick it out
when the time was right i closed my hand
i caught confidence, self belief, and passion
this is the day my mother told me
the world is mine
so now i'm telling you the world is yours

and after all the hurt you caused
i'm not bitter
i just hope you are able to love
someone else one day
you don't want to miss out
like you missed out on me

isn't it hard having deep thoughts but convincing yourself you have a shallow heart. not to hurt anyone but to protect yourself because you're afraid. you're afraid of having a love that's addicting and being with that special someone with a smile that's contagious to the point where you're weak and heavy hearted. isn't it easy being afraid of something so great that can end so devastating. falling for someone can result in ending underground while the other is flying above. the long hours in the shower and your tears blending in with water. the extra glass of wine at night to make your cloudy mind feel fine. and as time passes by, you will find your way holding your chin up with full confidence after letting go of someone that was a dream wrecker and fueled your nightmares. you will convince yourself that the deep roots of your soul are okay and you will have a love so powerful it can damage others but you'll choose to be easy and light with the once's that reflect beauty off of your shine.

it's not a competition
it's not a race
you should never feel the need to chase
you don't have to prove to someone
that you're better than the others
you shouldn't have to worry about
holding back parts of your heart
in order to be loved by another human
your heart is worthy
your mind has value

change,
the way green leaves turn brown
the way your skin gets wrinkles
or what people are fighting for in gun law

we are all changing as the days go by
maybe you fell out of love with yourself
because you fell in love with a dark soul
or maybe you just moved across the country
to follow your dreams
oh, change

life,
those long car rides because you feel like your head is going
to explode.
or maybe that cup of coffee that makes you feel warm and cozy.
you know when you feel like your walls are crashing in and
you can't explain how or why?
you know those moments where you can't catch your breath
because you are laughing too hard at the smallest things?
listen,
this is life
take it all in, roll down your windows, put your head outside,
close your eyes, and just
learn how to breathe.

these poems were my light and darkness of the past year. flashbacks on the floor of feeling empty and also flashbacks of being happy as ever. getting my heart broken has taught me to love every opportunity i am given more than ever. feel every emotion you feel in your heart and soul. scream your lungs out at a breathtaking view on your rough nights, or grab a blanket then go to the beach at 3am and stargaze until sunrise on your bright nights. i hope this book taught you to feel every emotion inside your body with a passion. i hope you found my heart through these words on paper. in some form, i hope i motivated your soul to ignite in power and love, to realize you have a heart of gold, and to find strength in yourself.

thank you for pausing your precious life to read bits and pieces of my story.

to be continued

YOU ARE ENOUGH

YOU ARE ENOUGH

YOU ARE ENOUGH

acknowledgment and love

to my past lovers, thank you for opening my heart and soul to a whole other capacity i never thought i was capable of. thank you for loving me and thank you for breaking me, i now found myself.

to my family, thanks for holding me up on the days where i didn't feel like standing, thanks for giving me strength and teaching me to have a wise mind in a shallow world. thanks for loving me unconditionally and believing in my creative mess of a mind.

to my mother, thanks for always being the hot coffee on my cold mornings. you managed to give me two hearts when you only had one. thanks for holding my hand in the darkness and thanks for hugging me during the sadness. your laugh lights up rooms and your presence always makes me feel like pure joy.

to quincie and candice, you are the greatest light i have ever discovered on earth. your love and comfort is endless and i could never put it into words how thankful i am for you two believing in me. the endless night drives with the windows down with you guys by my side will always mean the world to me. the simplicity of our friendship is what takes us thousands of miles into an entirely new world of love.

to courtney and jay, thanks for guiding me and lifting my imagination and making it into a real life book i can now hold in my hands. my entire heart and feelings are now all around the world touching others in their own unique way.

instagram: @benesqueda